This journal belongs to:

....

Date:

....

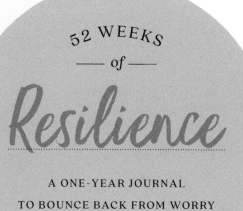

52 WEEKS

— *of* —

Resilience

A ONE-YEAR JOURNAL
TO BOUNCE BACK FROM WORRY
AND REDISCOVER PEACE

Ink &
Willow

Contents

Introduction

Worry often gives a small thing a big shadow.

SWEDISH PROVERB

There's no upside to worry. We lie awake at night imagining worst-case scenarios. We miss out on opportunities because we've become afraid of failure. We turn to coping mechanisms that turn into unhealthy habits that we then start worrying about.

Over the next fifty-two weeks, this journal will help you move from giving in to uneasiness to leaning on and trusting God. It is divided into four sections, each highlighting a simple practice you can apply to adjust your response to life's bumps. You'll learn how being *thankful, prayerful, thoughtful,* and *practical* can help you overcome anxious feelings. Each week, you'll find a Bible verse to read and meditate on, a question to reflect on and journal about, and an action prompt to help you let go of worry. Finally, at the end, you'll find a twelve-month "Daily Resilience Tracker," where you can begin the habit of recording one situation you encountered and how you bounced back.

This year resolve to switch your focus from the looming shadows of your problems to the greatness of the God who loves you.*

* Please note, this book is not intended to replace the advice of a trained psychologist or medical professional.

Thankful

▼▼▼▼▼▼▼▼▼

Gratitude doesn't change the scenery. It merely

washes clean the glass you look through

so you can clearly see the colors.

RICHELLE E. GOODRICH

As children, we learned to always say "thank you" when someone gave us a gift or did something kind for us. It's an excellent habit and, when expressed with sincerity, a word of appreciation can also convey respect, honor, and humility.

What we may not have perceived at a young age, however, is the benefit a grateful attitude has on our mind-sets and emotions. Many people see the connection between joy and gratitude as a one-way street. Sure, joy leads to gratitude, but how much sweeter it is when gratitude leads to joy!

When your default setting is "thankful," you change course from worry to gratitude because you've already decided to be joyful and peaceful without waiting for perfect circumstances. Worry doesn't stand a chance around you. When you choose gratitude, you're automatically a winner!

▲▲▲▲▲▲▲▲▲

WEEK 1

▼▼▼▼▼▼▼▼▼

Rejoice Always

Rejoice always, pray without ceasing, give
thanks in all circumstances; for this is the
will of God in Christ Jesus for you.

1 THESSALONIANS 5:16–18 (ESV)

Each day, you have twenty-four hours to do all the things you need and want to do. During each second you're awake, you also get to make choices about how you will think, feel, react, and behave. The more of that time you spend rejoicing, praying, and thanking, the less time you'll have left over to worry.

REFLECT

Why do you think God wants you to rejoice, pray, and give thanks on a continual basis?

....

....

....

....

....

....

....

....

....

....

....

....

....

....

....

....

....

....

....

....

....

....

....

....

....

....

....

....

....

....

....

RESPOND

WRITE PHRASES SUCH
AS "REJOICE!" OR "KEEP
PRAYING" ON SEVERAL
STICKY NOTES AND POST
THEM WHERE YOU CAN
SPOT THEM THROUGHOUT
THE DAY.

▼▼▼▼▼▼▼▼▼

A Firm Foundation

*Therefore let us be grateful for receiving a
kingdom that cannot be shaken, and thus let us
offer to God acceptable worship, with reverence
and awe, for our God is a consuming fire.*

HEBREWS 12:28-29 (ESV)

Unexpected challenges—a cancer diagnosis, the death of
a loved one, losing your job—can shake your world and
leave you feeling unsettled and scared. But remember, God's
promises, power, and provision are constant. Now there's
something to be thankful for!

REFLECT

What worries are you facing currently that you can turn over
to God?

....

....

....

....

....

....

....

....

....

....

....

....

....

....

....

....

....

....

....

....

....

....

....

....

....

....

....

....

RESPOND

TAKE FIVE MINUTES
TODAY TO LIST ALL THE
ATTRIBUTES OF GOD THAT
INSPIRE REVERENCE AND
AWE IN YOU. THANK HIM FOR
THESE, ONE BY ONE.

▼▼▼▼▼▼▼▼▼

Count Your Blessings

I will give thanks to the LORD with my whole heart;
I will recount all of your wonderful deeds.

PSALM 9:1 (ESV)

To worry is essentially to tell God we don't trust His ability—or willingness—to take care of us. If we are clutching on to worry in our heart while we're expressing thanks to God, that's half-hearted gratitude. We need to count our past blessings and trust Him with future ones.

REFLECT

Expressing gratitude verbally doesn't take much effort. When was the last time you were truly thankful and expressed your gratitude to God? What was the occasion and what was special about it? Write out a prayer of thanksgiving.

....

....

....

....

....

....

....

....

....

....

....

....

....

....

....

....

....

....

....

....

....

....

....

....

....

....

....

....

....

....

....

....

RESPOND

IF YOU'RE NOT FAMILIAR
WITH IT, LOOK UP THE
OLD HYMN "COUNT YOUR
BLESSINGS." LISTEN TO IT
SEVERAL TIMES THIS WEEK,
PAYING CLOSE ATTENTION
TO THE LYRICS. MAKE A NOTE
OF ANY INSPIRATION YOU
DRAW FROM IT.

WEEK 4

▼▼▼▼▼▼▼▼▼

More Than Enough

Taking the five loaves and the two fish and looking

up to heaven, he gave thanks and broke the loaves.

Then he . . . divided the two fish among them all.

MARK 6:41

The Bible has many examples of small faith rewarded with great results. Here we see Jesus thanking God for providing food for the crowd of thousands—through a young boy— *before* it was multiplied. God provided so much, there were even leftovers for the disciples to take home!

REFLECT

When in your life has God surprised you by providing much more than you needed? How did you feel?

....

....

....

....

....

....

....

....

....

....

....

....

....

....

....

....

....

....

....

....

....

....

....

....

....

....

....

RESPOND

ON AN INDEX CARD,
DRAW FIVE LOAVES OF BREAD
AND TWO FISH. ON THE BACK,
WRITE A PRAYER OF THANKS
FOR GOD'S PROVISION. KEEP
THE CARD WITH YOU AS A
REMINDER THAT GOD CARES
AND PROVIDES.

▼▼▼▼▼▼▼▼▼

Count It All Joy

Count it all joy, my brothers, when you meet

trials of various kinds, for you know that the

testing of your faith produces steadfastness.

JAMES 1:2-3 (ESV)

Feeling thankful for problems is not only countercultural but it's also counterintuitive. It doesn't seem logical! Yet James lets us in on a marvelous secret in this passage: Difficulties make us stronger. So, even when you're worried, there's always a reason to rejoice.

REFLECT

What's your instinctive response when a new problem pops up at home, in a relationship, or at work? Think of a current problem you are worried about and write out how you can reframe it as a blessing.

....

....

....

....

....

....

....
....
....
....
....
....
....
....
....
....
....
....
....
....
....
....
....

RESPOND

USE A BLANK THANK-YOU
CARD TO WRITE A NOTE TO GOD,
THANKING HIM FOR SPECIFIC
DIFFICULTIES HE BROUGHT YOU
THROUGH SAFELY IN THE PAST
AND NOTING HOW THOSE TRIALS
STRENGTHENED YOUR FAITH.
THANK HIM FOR HOW HE
WILL BE WITH YOU
IN FUTURE TRIALS.

▼▼▼▼▼▼▼▼▼

Called to Peace

Let the peace of Christ rule in your hearts,

since as members of one body you were

called to peace. And be thankful.

COLOSSIANS 3:15

Christ's peace isn't simply a nice feeling. It's an authority that should preside over everything else in our hearts. Peace and apprehension cannot coexist, and neither can thankfulness and discord.

REFLECT

Think of a tense relationship that makes you feel anxious. What about it makes you feel that way? Write out a prayer now, asking God to cover you in future interactions with that person.

....

....

....

....

....

....

....

....
....
....
....
....
....
....
....
....
....
....
....
....
....
....
....
....
....
....
....
....
....
....

RESPOND

THIS WEEK RESOLVE TO
TAKE THE FIRST STEP
TOWARD PEACE—SHOOT
A TEXT, SEND A CARD, OR
SCHEDULE A PHONE CALL
WITH SOMEONE YOU HAVE
BEEN AT ODDS
WITH RECENTLY.

▼▼▼▼▼▼▼▼

The Glad Game Strategy

The LORD has done it this very day; let

us rejoice today and be glad.

PSALM 118:24

Some days, gratitude comes easily. Everything's coming up roses, the house is clean, and the bills are paid. But what about the days the fridge breaks down, you lose your wallet, and the dog throws up? Is it possible to still find something to "rejoice and be glad" about? It might not fix the situation, but it might give you the lift you need to make it through the day.

REFLECT

How can you find reasons to be glad, no matter what circumstances you find yourself in? Think of one unfortunate situation you've experienced recently and write down how you can be glad anyway, simply because God is still good.

....

....

....

....

....

....

....
....
....
....
....
....
....
....
....
....
....
....
....
....
....
....
....
....

RESPOND

IF YOU'RE NOT FAMILIAR
WITH THE GLAD GAME FROM
POLLYANNA, LOOK IT UP ONLINE.
BETTER YET, BORROW OR
PURCHASE POLLYANNA (THE
BOOK OR MOVIE) AND TRY TO
IMPLEMENT HER APPROACH
IN YOUR DAILY LIFE.

▼▼▼▼▼▼▼▼▼

Safe in His Hand

So do not fear, for I am with you; do not be dismayed,
for I am your God. I will strengthen you and help you;
I will uphold you with my righteous right hand.

ISAIAH 41:10

Walking in the dark or traveling in an unfamiliar area
becomes a lot less scary when we have a friend with us. We
appreciate the companionship and security. In the same way,
knowing God is with us can help us face the unknowns ahead
of us without fear.

REFLECT

What worries does it feel like you are currently carrying on
your own? What is something or someone who can help
remind you that God is with you and that you are not alone?

....

....

....

....

....

....

....

....

....

....

....

....

....

....

....

....

....

....

....

....

....

....

....

RESPOND

ON A PIECE OF PAPER, TRACE
AROUND YOUR HAND. WRITE
ISAIAH 41:10 INSIDE THE SHAPE,
THANKING GOD AS YOU DO,
REMEMBERING THAT HE IS THERE
TO HELP YOU. TAKE A PHOTO
AND USE IT AS YOUR PHONE
BACKGROUND TO REMIND YOU
YOU'RE NOT ALONE.

WEEK 9

▼▼▼▼▼▼▼▼▼

The Trees of the Field

You will go out in joy and be led forth in peace; the

mountains and hills will burst into song before you,

and all the trees of the field will clap their hands.

ISAIAH 55:12

Nothing in nature is self-sufficient—and nature knows that.
From the tallest mountain to the tiniest gnat, everything points
to God as a loving and attentive Creator.

REFLECT

From the smallest creature to the largest tree, what are some
things creation has to be thankful about?

....

....

....

....

....

....

....

....

....

....
....
....
....
....
....
....
....
....
....
....
....
....
....
....
....
....
....
....
....
....

RESPOND

ON A LARGE PIECE OF PAPER, DRAW A TREE WITH BARE BRANCHES. THROUGHOUT THE WEEK, DRAW LEAVES WHENEVER YOU REMEMBER A BLESSING. LABEL THE LEAF AND SAY A QUICK PRAYER OF THANKS. WHENEVER YOU FEEL ANXIOUS, READ THE LEAVES!

WEEK 10

♥♥♥♥♥♥♥♥♥

Who God Is

And he will be called Wonderful Counselor, Mighty

God, Everlasting Father, Prince of Peace.

ISAIAH 9:6

The more we know someone, the easier it is to discern how much we can trust him or her. When we know our God, we know who stands with us in the trials.

REFLECT

Make a list of all the things God *is* (not *does*) for which you're thankful. Write a sentence or two about why this list should help relieve your worries.

....

....

....

....

....

....

....

....

....

....
....
....
....
....
....
....
....
....
....
....
....
....
....
....
....
....
....
....
....
....
....
....
....
....
....

▼▼▼▼▼▼▼▼

People Need People

At the sight of these people Paul thanked
God and was encouraged.

ACTS 28:15

On their way to Rome, Paul and the other apostles met some believers who invited them to spend a week with them (Acts 28). Paul recognized the blessing these believers—nameless to us today—were and he responded with gratitude.

REFLECT

How does it encourage you when people—whether loved ones or strangers—reach out to you with warmth and graciousness? Write about a time you experienced this and how it made you feel.

....

....

....

....

....

....

....

....

....
....
....
....
....
....
....
....
....
....
....
....
....
....
....
....
....
....
....
....
....

RESPOND

THINK OF THREE PEOPLE
WHO HAVE REASSURED YOU
DURING DIFFICULT TIMES.
TAKE TIME THIS WEEK
TO CALL THEM OR MAIL A
NOTE, THANKING THEM FOR
ENCOURAGING YOU.

Rain from Heaven

Yet he has not left himself without testimony: He
has shown kindness by giving you rain from heaven
and crops in their seasons; he provides you with
plenty of food and fills your hearts with joy.

ACTS 14:17

We learn to trust people when they keep their word and deliver on their promises. We can trust God because, since the beginning of time, He has demonstrated His love and kindness—even promising rain. Rain can seem like more of a nuisance than a blessing until we consider how it nourishes the earth that sustains us.

REFLECT

How is the earth's ecosystem a testimony of God's kindness and care for you? Make a list of things in nature that bring you a sense of gratitude or calm.

....

....

....

....

....

....
....
....
....
....
....
....
....
....
....
....
....
....
....
....

....

....

....

....

....

....

....

RESPOND

GO OUT INTO NATURE THIS
WEEK. (IF YOU ARE UNABLE
TO GET TO NATURE, FIND A
COMFORTING NATURE SCENE
ON THE INTERNET OR IN A
MAGAZINE.) WHAT BLESSINGS
CAN YOU FIND OUTSIDE, NO
MATTER THE WEATHER?

▼▼▼▼▼▼▼▼▼

He Will Provide

Keep your lives free from the love of money and be

content with what you have, because God has said,

"Never will I leave you; never will I forsake you."

HEBREWS 13:5

Nowhere does the Bible condemn being wealthy, but it warns against greed and discontent. The love of money afflicts billionaires and those living in poverty. No amount of cash can satisfy our soul's cravings and bring us serenity. Only God can fill that hole.

REFLECT

When it comes to your financial situation, what areas cause you the most anxiety? Where do you have trouble trusting God to provide?

....

....

....

....

....

....

....

....

....

....

....

....

....

....

....

....

....

....

....

....

....

....

....

....

....

....

RESPOND

TAKE A LOOK AT THE MONEY
YOU HAVE AVAILABLE RIGHT
NOW. COMMIT EACH DOLLAR TO
THE LORD AND ASK HIM TO EASE
YOUR FEARS, HELP YOU TRUST HIS
PROVISION, AND TEACH YOU
TO BE A GOOD STEWARD OF
WHAT HE HAS GIVEN YOU.

Be Pray

▼▼▼▼▼▼▼▼▼

No one can pray and worry at the same time.

MAX LUCADO

When we tell God the things we're worried about, our "Amen" should serve as a signature that transfers ownership of the problem to Him and that our worries now rest at His feet. Unfortunately, many of us pick them right back up and carry those burdens long after we've said "Amen."

Prayer is a privilege like no other. It gives us direct and immediate access to the Creator of the universe and the King of kings, the God who wants to be not only our Lord but also our Father and our Friend . . . the Lover of our souls.

While modern technology may allow us to quickly exchange text messages or have a video chat with friends, even the best app cannot compare to the clear, uninterrupted, high-speed, private communication we can have with God.

These truths about prayer should already strengthen our minds and hearts . . . even before we've entered the presence of God to leave our burdens with Him.

▲▲▲▲▲▲▲▲▲

WEEK 14

▼▼▼▼▼▼▼▼▼

Tell God About It

Do not be anxious about anything, but in everything
by prayer and supplication with thanksgiving let your
requests be made known to God. And the peace of
God, which surpasses all understanding, will guard
your hearts and your minds in Christ Jesus.

PHILIPPIANS 4:6–7 (ESV)

There isn't a single situation in your life that is either too big
or too small for God. He is powerful enough and loving
enough to handle it all. He wants you to come to Him with any
worry you have.

REFLECT

What small things are you worried about that you think are
too insignificant to pray about?

....

....

....

....

....

....

....

....

....

....

....

....

....

....

....

....

....

....

....

....

....

....

....

....

....

....

....

....

....

....

RESPOND

THIS WEEK, REMEMBER
TO PRAY FOR BOTH THE BIG
AND THE LITTLE THINGS—
BECAUSE GOD CARES FOR
ALL OF THEM.

WEEK 15

▼▼▼▼▼▼▼▼▼

Overflow

May the God of hope fill you with all joy and peace
as you trust in him, so that you may overflow
with hope by the power of the Holy Spirit.

ROMANS 15:13

Whatever you fill a container with, that's what will spill out
when you squeeze it or tip it over. Similarly, our lives can
overflow with bitterness, anxiety, or anger . . . or with joy,
peace, and hope! It depends on what we're filled with. Being
intentional about what we fill our minds with ensures that in
times of stress, our hearts can still overflow with cheerfulness
and hope through the Holy Spirit.

REFLECT

If you were a cup that started overflowing, what would pour
out today? Why?

....

....

....

....

....

....

....

....

....

....

....

....

....

....

....

....

....

....

....

....

....

....

....

....

....

....

....

....

....

....

RESPOND

THE NEXT TIME YOU POUR
YOURSELF A DRINK, OFFER A
BRIEF PRAYER TO GOD ASKING
HIM TO EMPTY YOUR HEART OF
WORRY AND TO FILL IT INSTEAD
WITH HOPE. TRY TO MAKE A
HABIT OF THIS EXERCISE.

Only One Thing

You are worried and upset about many things, but

few things are needed—or indeed only one.

LUKE 10:41-42

It's easy to feel frazzled and disconnected when we're trying to do too many things at once. This was never God's design for us, as we see in the story of Martha and Mary, and in the way Jesus lived His life. Even when we are experiencing so much stress that we feel as though we haven't been able to get anything done, if we set aside time to sit at the feet of Jesus, we have accomplished the most important thing of all.

REFLECT

Think of a time when you experienced extreme peace and rest—maybe it was even amid chaos. How might you re-create the comfort of that experience in your daily life?

....

....

....

....

....

....

....
....
....
....
....
....
....
....
....
....
....
....
....
....
....
....
....
....
....
....
....

RESPOND

READ LUKE 10:38–42 SLOWLY,
EVEN A FEW TIMES. PUT ASIDE
FIFTEEN MINUTES TODAY AND
SIT QUIETLY IN GOD'S PRESENCE.
ASK HIM TO SPEAK TO YOU
AND TO HELP YOU LISTEN AS
MARY DID INSTEAD OF
FRETTING LIKE MARTHA.

WEEK 17

▼▼▼▼▼▼▼▼▼

Let It Go

Cast all your anxiety on him because he cares for you.

1 PETER 5:7

God did not set up a complicated submission process to go through when we want to submit our worries to Him. We're told to *cast* our anxieties on Him. In other words, fling, toss, hurl, pitch, or drop them, without ceremony or hesitation!

REFLECT

What are the concerns you are hanging on to that are preventing you from fully trusting God? What process do you go to when you're trying to let go of worry? Is it working for you? Commit to casting your worries on God the moment they come to mind.

....

....

....

....

....

....

....

....

. . . .

. . . .

. . . .

. . . .

. . . .

. . . .

. . . .

. . . .

. . . .

. . . .

. . . .

. . . .

. . . .

. . . .

. . . .

. . . .

. . . .

. . . .

. . . .

RESPOND

FIND AN EMPTY JAR
AND LABEL IT "GOD CARES."
WHENEVER YOU FEEL ANXIOUS
ABOUT SOMETHING, WRITE THE
CONCERN ON A SLIP OF PAPER,
CRUMPLE IT UP, AND DROP IT INTO
THE JAR WHILE YOU THANK GOD
THAT HE CARES ABOUT YOU
AND YOUR CONCERNS.

▼▼▼▼▼▼▼▼▼

But I will sing of your strength, in the morning

I will sing of your love; for you are my

fortress, my refuge in times of trouble.

PSALM 59:16

What we allow our minds and hearts to dwell on first thing in the morning can set the tone for the rest of the day. Starting off the day with a song of worship—rejoicing in God's strength and love as a form of prayerful praise—is a great way to remember He is there for us in every situation.

REFLECT

When do you most feel like singing—when you're sad or when you're happy? How does singing affect your mood?

....

....

....

....

....

....

....

....

....

....

....

....

....

....

....

....

....

....

....

....

....

....

....

....

....

....

....

....

....

....

....

RESPOND

MAKE A POINT OF SINGING OR
LISTENING TO WORSHIP SONGS
A LITTLE BIT EVERY DAY THIS
WEEK, EVEN IF IT'S JUST IN THE
SHOWER OR CAR. DON'T WORRY
ABOUT WHAT OTHERS THINK—
JUST PRAISE GOD!

▼▼▼▼▼▼▼▼▼

Lighten Your Load

Take my yoke upon you and learn from me, for I am
gentle and humble in heart, and you will find rest for
your souls. For my yoke is easy and my burden is light.

MATTHEW 11:29–30

For an intangible, invisible emotion, worry can sure weigh us down. Sometimes the pressure is so great we feel like we're being crushed, and even breathing takes too much effort. There is a solution, and His name is Jesus.

REFLECT

How do you cope when uncertainty and pain close in on you and your heart feels heavy? Why do you think that is your initial reaction? Have you found that it helps you overcome some of that worry?

....

....

....

....

....

....

....

▼▼▼▼▼▼▼▼▼

Pray for Others

I urge, then, first of all, that petitions, prayers,

intercession and thanksgiving be made for all people.

1 TIMOTHY 2:1

Praying for our needs can help put our minds at ease, but God wants us to pray for others, too. It is a way to serve them and also allows us a short break from focusing on our own concerns.

REFLECT

Who are the people you worry about the most, and why? Who are at least two people you can pray for this week? In what specific areas can you pray for them?

....

....

....

....

....

....

....

....

....

....

....

....

....

....

....

....

....

....

....

....

....

....

....

....

....

RESPOND

DEDICATE ONE PAGE OF
A NOTEBOOK TO EACH PERSON
ON YOUR PRAYER LIST.
AS YOU PRAY FOR THEM, JOT
DOWN WORDS OF THANKS OR
PETITION. OR TRY THE "PRAYING
IN COLOR" METHOD. (SEARCH
ONLINE FOR IDEAS.)

▼▼▼▼▼▼▼▼▼

Fear No Evil

Even though I walk through the darkest valley,
I will fear no evil, for you are with me; your
rod and your staff, they comfort me.

PSALM 23:4

Some of us will never experience the dark valleys others have to go through, but our own struggles can be just as scary if we believe we are alone and helpless. Acknowledging God's presence by bringing our fears to Him can sustain us.

REFLECT

How have you been inspired by Christians who continue to trust God through times of persecution or great loss? What do you think some of their fears may have been? How do you think they overcame the worry and fear?

....

....

....

....

....

....

....

....

....

....

....

....

....

....

....

....

....

....

....

....

....

....

....

....

....

RESPOND

ON A PIECE OF PAPER OR AN INDEX CARD, REWRITE PSALM 23:4 AND MAKE IT PERSONAL BY ACKNOWLEDGING WHAT YOU'RE WORRIED ABOUT AND WHY YOU WILL NOT BE AFRAID. CARRY IT WITH YOU THIS WEEK.

▼▼▼▼▼▼▼▼▼

Trust in the Lord

Trust in the LORD with all your heart and lean not
on your own understanding; in all your ways submit
to him, and he will make your paths straight.

PROVERBS 3:5-6

For most of us, when we were kids, there was something reassuring and freeing about having our parents make decisions for us. We felt safe because we knew they were looking out for us. We can rely on God in the same way. Turn to Him when you are faced with big decisions and need reassurance.

REFLECT

Describe a time you could see God looking out for you in a difficult situation. What were the ways you felt His presence and guidance?

....

....

....

....

....

....

....

....

....

....

....

....

....

....

....

....

....

....

....

....

....

....

....

....

....

....

....

....

RESPOND

ON A PIECE OF PAPER,
CONFESS TO GOD ANY
PROBLEMS YOU'VE BEEN TRYING
TO SOLVE ALONE, AND TUCK
THAT PAPER INTO THE BACK OF
THIS JOURNAL. USE IT AS
A REMINDER TO TRUST
THAT GOD WILL TAKE
CARE OF IT.

WEEK 23

▼▼▼▼▼▼▼▼▼

Like a Tree

But blessed is the one who trusts in the LORD,

whose confidence is in him. They will be like a tree

planted by the water. . . . It has no worries in a

year of drought and never fails to bear fruit.

JEREMIAH 17:7–8

Too many of us walk around with to-do lists that don't
necessarily reflect God's expectations of us. By praying, we
are learning to trust and obey—to put our confidence in Him
instead of in our own abilities and efforts.

REFLECT

What are some of the things you're trying to do while solely
relying on your own strength? List some of the expectations
you have put on yourself. When you reflect on Scripture, what
are the expectations God has for you?

....

....

....

....

....

....

....

....

....

....

....

....

....

....

....

....

....

....

....

....

....

RESPOND

IF YOU CAN, GO FOR A WALK
WHERE YOU CAN ENJOY THE
BEAUTY OF CREATION. THINK ABOUT
ALL THE SPECIFIC WAYS GOD TAKES
CARE OF THE PLANTS AND THE
FLOWERS OF THE FIELD. ASK HIM
TO HELP YOU HAVE CONFIDENCE
IN HIS ABILITIES INSTEAD
OF SOLELY YOUR OWN.

▼▼▼▼▼▼▼▼

Short and Simple

When I am afraid, I put my trust in you.

PSALM 56:3

Prayers don't need to be long to be meaningful or powerful. In today's verse, just ten words say enough. David's prayer is one you can remember and lift up at any moment.

REFLECT

Before he became king, young David faced lions and giants, never doubting God was with him. How can you have that kind of courage?

....

....

....

....

....

....

....

....

....

....

....

....

....

....

....

....

....

....

....

....

....

....

....

....

....

....

....

....

RESPOND

FIND A SMOOTH STONE
AND WRITE "TRUST GOD"
ON IT. KEEP THE STONE
ON YOUR DESK OR IN YOUR
POCKET AND REPEAT
PSALM 56:3 WHENEVER
YOU FEEL AFRAID.

WEEK 25

▼▼▼▼▼▼▼▼▼

Get Closer

Come near to God and he will come near

to you. Wash your hands, you sinners, and

purify your hearts, you double-minded.

JAMES 4:8

God invites us into deeper intimacy with Him, but it can
be difficult to experience that intimacy when our worries
monopolize our attention. When we consistently spend time
in prayer, our hearts become right with Him and our minds
can be more resilient to worry.

REFLECT

Make a list of all the worries your mind is focused on right
now. When these worries come knocking, what steps can you
take to redirect your attention toward intimacy with God?

....

....

....

....

....

....

....
....
....
....
....
....
....
....
....
....
....
....
....
....
....
....
....
....
....

RESPOND

USING THE LIST YOU
CREATED ABOVE, FIND AN
ATTRIBUTE OF GOD THAT
IS THE ANTIDOTE FOR EACH
WORRY. EVERY TIME YOU
WASH YOUR HANDS THIS
WEEK, REMIND YOURSELF
THAT GOD IS NEAR.

▼▼▼▼▼▼▼▼▼

Even the Little Things

Are not two sparrows sold for a penny? And not one of

them will fall to the ground apart from your Father. But

even the hairs of your head are all numbered. Fear not,

therefore; you are of more value than many sparrows.

MATTHEW 10:29–31 (ESV)

God knows—and *cares*—about everything in this world, whether it is a tiny bird that falls from the sky or the number of hairs on your head. If he cares about those little things, think about how much more he cares about you!

REFLECT

What are some needs you worry God won't meet or care about, maybe because you're afraid they're too small or insignificant?

....

....

....

....

....

....

....

....
....
....
....
....
....
....
....
....
....
....
....
....
....
....
....

RESPOND

PRAY FOR EACH OF THE
WORRIES ABOVE, ONE AT
A TIME. THEN CROSS OUT
EACH WORRY ON THE LIST
AS A COMMITMENT TO
TRUST GOD WITH THEM.

▼▽▼▼▽▼▼▽▼

Worry compounds the futility of being trapped on

a dead-end street. Thinking opens new avenues.

CULLEN HIGHTOWER

H uman beings often act on impulse, propelled by our emotions. But even when we're overcome by "all the feels," it's our thoughts and attitudes and beliefs that generally influence our behavior and choices. Unlike animals, who respond instinctively, we have the capacity to reason and reflect, to examine and evaluate.

When our thinking is clear and our belief system is sound, when we've learned God's truths and His promises, we guard ourselves against anxiety and distress. Sure, we will still feel scared at times. We'll experience grief, uncertainty, and disappointment, but pausing to think things through helps us regain our footing and will give us strength.

▲▲▲▲▲▲▲▲▲

▾ ▾ ▾ ▾ ▾ ▾ ▾ ▾ ▾

Rest Your Mind

You drench [the land's] furrows and level its ridges;
you soften it with showers and bless its crops.

PSALM 65:10

What is it about a shower that makes us feel like we've hit a
"Reset" button? More than the fact that we're washing away
dirt and grease, it's the sensation of refreshment. Whether
you prefer a bracing cold shower or a steaming one, a shower
can help you clear your head and remind you to breathe,
especially if you use the time for reflection.

REFLECT

What are some ways you wash away the worry and stress?
How does it differ from when God washes away the worry and
stress? How often do you turn to Him for that refreshment?

....

....

....

....

....

....

....

....

....

....

....

....

....

....

....

....

....

....

....

....

....

....

....

....

....

....

....

....

.... **RESPOND**

.... USE YOUR SHOWER TIMES
TO REMEMBER PSALM 65:10
.... AND GOD'S PROMISES INSTEAD
OF DWELLING ON YOUR WORRIES.
.... DECLARE YOUR RESTROOM A
WORRY-FREE ROOM OF REST
.... FOR YOUR MIND AS WELL.
(PUT UP A SIGN IF
.... YOU NEED TO!)

....

▼▼▼▼▼▼▼▼▼

Can You Imagine?

Now to him who is able to do immeasurably
more than all we ask or imagine, according
to his power that is at work within us.

EPHESIANS 3:20

You're probably used to people over-promising and under-delivering. The Bible tells us and shows us that the Creator delivers on His promises and exceeds our expectations. Praise be to God!

REFLECT

What do you think of when you hear the phrase "immeasurably more"? In what area of your life are you hoping God will do immeasurably more for you?

....

....

....

....

....

....

....

....

....
....
....
....
....
....
....
....
....
....
....
....
....
....
....
....
....
....
....
....
....
....

RESPOND

CLOSE YOUR EYES AND
TAKE AT LEAST THREE
MINUTES TO REFLECT ON
GOD DOING "IMMEASURABLY
MORE" THAN YOU CAN
IMAGINE. BREATHE IN GOD'S
STRENGTH, AND BREATHE
OUT YOUR WEAKNESS.

▼▼▼▼▼▼▼▼▼

A Material World

*Therefore I tell you, do not worry about your
life, what you will eat or drink; or about your
body, what you will wear. Is not life more than
food, and the body more than clothes?*

MATTHEW 6:25

Perhaps you don't worry whether you will be able to eat tomorrow, but you may feel a pinch when your rent is due or the kids need something for school or extracurricular activities. You may be able to afford new shoes, but what about your student loan or your next car payment? Sometimes, the more stuff we have, the more stress we have, too. We should remember that God knows and cares for all our needs.

REFLECT

Who has been an example to you of trusting God when resources are limited? What about their response can you emulate when you are in a similar situation?

....

....

....

....

WRITE OUT MATTHEW 6:25
ON SEVERAL PIECES OF PAPER.
PLACE THESE REMINDERS IN YOUR
POCKETS, ON YOUR FRIDGE, YOUR
BATHROOM MIRROR, YOUR CAR'S
DASH—PLACES YOU SEE OR USE
EVERY DAY—AND ASK GOD TO
EASE YOUR MIND ABOUT
YOUR DAILY NEEDS.

WEEK 30

▼▼▼▼▼▼▼▼▼

Such Things

Finally, brothers and sisters, whatever is true, whatever
is noble, whatever is right, whatever is pure, whatever
is lovely, whatever is admirable—if anything is
excellent or praiseworthy—think about such things.

PHILIPPIANS 4:8

During a typical day, where do your thoughts tend to go? The
path of least resistance seems to pull our minds toward worst-
case scenarios, suspicion, doubt, and resentment, leaving us
exhausted and grumpy. Remember, you can always choose
what you think about.

REFLECT

What are eight things, events, or people that are true, noble,
right, pure, lovely, admirable, excellent, and praiseworthy
in your life right now? How do they embody those
specific traits?

....

....

....

....

....

....

....

....

....

....

....

....

....

....

....

....

....

....

....

....

....

....

....

....

RESPOND

THIS WEEK, WHEN YOU COME ACROSS SOMETHING TRUE, NOBLE, RIGHT, AND SO FORTH, SNAP A PICTURE WITH YOUR PHONE. WHEN YOUR THOUGHTS TURN TOWARD WORRY, PULL UP ONE OF THOSE PICTURES TO REFOCUS YOUR MIND.

The Lord Is . . .

The Lord is my light and my salvation—

whom shall I fear? The Lord is the stronghold

of my life—of whom shall I be afraid?

PSALM 27:1

There's a saying that, instead of telling God how big your problems are, you should tell your problems how big your God is. We too easily forget that no one and nothing that threatens us escapes God's notice or is beyond His power to save us.

REFLECT

List the problems about which you need reminders that God is bigger than. Next to each worry, write out "God is bigger."

....

....

....

....

....

....

....

....

RESPOND

IN YOUR BIBLE,
GO THROUGH PSALM 27,
HIGHLIGHTING IN ONE COLOR
ALL THE REQUESTS MADE, IN
A SECOND COLOR ALL THE
PROMISES OF WHAT GOD WILL DO,
AND IN A THIRD COLOR ALL
THE RESPONSES OF THOSE
WHO TRUSTS HIM.

He Is with You

The LORD your God is with you, the Mighty

Warrior who saves. He will take great delight

in you; in his love he will no longer rebuke you,

but will rejoice over you with singing.

ZEPHANIAH 3:17

Amid the battle, we often focus on the unknown. But the Bible reminds us that the Mighty Warrior is with us. God fights alongside us and on our behalf.

REFLECT

Where does your focus normally lie when faced with the unknown? What happens when you instead direct your gaze toward the Mighty Warrior who saves?

....

....

....

....

....

....

....

....
....
....
....
....
....
....
....
....
....
....
....
....
....
....
....
....

....

.... $RESPOND$

....

....   MEMORIZE ZEPHANIAH 3:17
....   THIS WEEK AND SHARE IT
                                                         WITH AT LEAST TWO FRIENDS
....   WHO ARE STRUGGLING
                                                         WITH WORRY OR
....   DISCOURAGEMENT.

....

....

WEEK 33

▼▼▼▼▼▼▼▼▼

It's About Time

Who of you by worrying can add

a single hour to your life?

LUKE 12:25

Like a hamster wheel for a hamster, worry can keep us busy, but it isn't a productive use of our energy, time, or imagination. It doesn't take us anywhere and doesn't even feel good, so why do we keep worrying?

REFLECT

Instead of focusing on a persistent worry, write out three things you are excited about or looking forward to.

....

....

....

....

....

....

....

....

....

....

....

....

....

....

....

....

....

....

....

....

....

....

....

....

....

....

....

....

....

....

....

....

RESPOND

AS YOU PREPARE FOR BED
EACH NIGHT, MAKE IT A HABIT
TO CONCENTRATE YOUR SENSES
ON THE PRESENT MOMENT—THE
SIGHTS, SOUNDS, SMELLS, AND
TEXTURES OF HOME. APPRECIATE
THE LAST PRECIOUS MINUTES
OF THE DAY INSTEAD OF
WORRYING ABOUT
THE FUTURE.

WEEK 34

▼▼▼▼▼▼▼▼▼

Fix Your Thoughts

Therefore, holy brothers and sisters, who share in the
heavenly calling, fix your thoughts on Jesus, whom
we acknowledge as our apostle and high priest.

HEBREWS 3:1

We board planes and trains without worrying whether the
pilot or conductor knows how to get us to our destination.
Trusting Jesus with our lives should come even more
naturally. It can help to turn our thoughts toward Him when
we need help.

REFLECT

What are some things you trust without question? Why do
you trust them?

....

....

....

....

....

....

....

....

RESPOND

THE NEXT TIME YOU
ARE DRIVING, COMMUTING,
OR TRAVELING, THINK ABOUT
THE TRUST YOU SUBCONSCIOUSLY
HAVE IN YOUR MODE OF
TRANSPORTATION. THANK GOD
FOR BEING EVEN MORE RELIABLE
IN GUIDING YOU THROUGH
THE DIFFERENT POINTS
IN YOUR LIFE.

▼▼▼▼▼▼▼▼▼

God Loves You

There is no fear in love. But perfect love drives
out fear, because fear has to do with punishment.
The one who fears is not made perfect in love.

1 JOHN 4:18

So much of our tendency to worry is rooted in fear of the unknown. We don't know how a situation will unfold so we feel as though it's out of control. It may be out of *our* control, but not God's. The more we rest in His love, the less power fear has over us.

REFLECT

When a situation scares you and you start to worry, how can it help to reflect on God's love and promises?

....

....

....

....

....

....

....

....

I ♡ you
:)

....
....
....
....
....
....
....
....
....
....
....
....
....
....
....
....
....
....
....
....
....
....

RESPOND

ON A STICKY NOTE OR BLANK
CARD, DRAW THE OUTLINE OF A
HEART IN RED AND THEN WRITE
"THERE IS NO FEAR IN LOVE" IN
THE CENTER. PUT THIS LOVE NOTE
ON YOUR FRIDGE OR MIRROR
AS A REGULAR REMINDER
THAT YOU DON'T NEED
TO WORRY.

WEEK 36

▼▼▼▼▼▼▼▼▼

Prudence Pays

The simple believes everything, but the

prudent gives thought to his steps.

PROVERBS 14:15 (ESV)

We live in a world where news is broadcast within seconds of it happening, and reactions—emojis, likes, and upvotes—are just as quick. In mere minutes, a video goes viral, heated debates escalate, and scandals destroy families. Next time you're scrolling the internet, remember that Proverbs instructs us to be prudent. Let your first response be to take a step back rather than immediately react. Let's hit "Pause" for a moment.

REFLECT

When you hear sensational news that causes widespread panic, how do you react? Do you follow the crowd, or do you take time to get the facts and plan your next move?

....

....

....

....

....

....
....
....
....
....
....
....
....
....
....
....
....
....
....

RESPOND

PROMISE YOURSELF TO IGNORE
THE IMPULSE TO IMMEDIATELY
SHARE OR RESPOND TO UPSETTING
NEWS YOU SEE ON SOCIAL MEDIA.
INSTEAD, WAIT UNTIL YOU'VE
PRAYED ABOUT IT AND DONE
SOME RESEARCH.

▼▼▼▼▼▼▼▼▼

Take the Test

Search me, God, and know my heart; test

me and know my anxious thoughts.

PSALM 139:23

Sharing our deepest secrets with a trusted loved one can be liberating, and it also gives us an opportunity to receive good advice or support. How comforting then to realize that God already knows our thoughts and feelings, and the things we're anxious about, even better than we understand them ourselves.

REFLECT

Read and reflect on all of Psalm 139. Write out the verses that especially resonate with you. Why do they comfort you?

....

....

....

....

....

....

....

....

....

....

....

....

....

....

....

....

....

....

....

....

....

....

....

....

....

....

....

....

....

RESPOND

WHO IS A TRUSTED FRIEND
OR LOVED ONE THAT YOU
CAN TURN TO IN TIMES OF
TROUBLE? SEND A CARD OR
CALL THAT PERSON THIS WEEK,
JUST TO LET THEM KNOW YOU
CARE ABOUT THEM.

WEEK 38

▼▼▼▼▼▼▼▼▼

Day and Night

Keep this Book of the Law always on your lips;
meditate on it day and night, so that you may
be careful to do everything written in it. Then
you will be prosperous and successful.

JOSHUA 1:8

Video tutorials and how-to books can teach us everything
from applying eyeliner to retiling bathroom floors to making
the perfect Pavlova. We invest a lot of time and money to learn
how to improve our lives. Imagine how life-giving it would be
to put the same effort into studying the words of the Bible!

REFLECT

Write out some verses you are familiar with and find yourself
repeating regularly.

....

....

....

....

....

....

....

....

....

....

....

....

....

....

....

....

....

....

....

....

....

....

....

....

....

....

....

....

RESPOND

CHOOSE A SIMPLE BUT
MEANINGFUL BIBLE VERSE
(THE ONES IN THIS BOOK ARE
GREAT OPTIONS!) AND MEMORIZE
IT. RECITE IT TO YOURSELF
WHENEVER YOUR MIND TURNS
TOWARD WORRY.

▼▼▼▼▼▼▼▼▼

Please God (Only)

Am I now trying to win the approval of human beings,

or of God? Or am I trying to please people? If I were still

trying to please people, I would not be a servant of Christ.

GALATIANS 1:10

The compulsive need for the approval of others seems to be a common ailment among women, especially Christian women. We worry about the opinions of others in every area of our lives. But the Bible reassures us we only have to focus on pleasing God.

REFLECT

In what areas of your life do you tend to want to please others first? What would it look like to please God in those areas instead of others?

....

....

....

....

....

....

....

....
....
....
....
....
....
....
....
....
....
....
....
....
....
....
....
....
....

RESPOND

TAKE SOME TIME TO MEMORIZE
COLOSSIANS 3:23. THE NEXT
TIME YOU ARE TEMPTED TO
PLEASE OTHERS, USE THAT
VERSE TO REMIND YOU THAT
GOD IS THE ONLY ONE YOU
HAVE TO PLEASE.

Be

Practical

▼▼▼▼▼▼▼▼▼

If you can't sleep, then get up and do something

instead of lying there worrying. It's the worry

that gets you, not the lack of sleep.

DALE CARNEGIE

None of us can control everything that happens in our lives, and often trying to take control just makes things worse. What we *can* control, however, is our response to difficult situations. With a little determination— and practice—we can outsmart the weaselly worry that invades our thoughts and emotions. We can be proactive and practical, taking steps to stop anxious thoughts in their tracks.

Wallowing in worry is the easier choice but doing so turns a manageable situation into something painful and distracting. That doesn't mean ignoring or denying how we feel. Rather, it means having the courage to face the problem head-on and telling it you're not nearly ready to give in. Let's do this!

▲▲▲▲▲▲▲▲▲

▼▼▼▼▼▼▼▼

Lessons from the Past

Let this be recorded for a generation to come, so that

a people yet to be created may praise the Lord.

PSALM 102:18 (ESV)

Each generation has moments of trials and moments of overcoming. It's easy to disregard or forget that our problems are not unique to us in the present. We can look back to learn from those who have gone before us and use their experience as a roadmap to adapt and emerge from challenges stronger than we were before.

REFLECT

What's a story from a parent, grandparent, or other family member that demonstrates their ability to overcome difficult circumstances? What steps did that person take to come back even stronger than before?

....

....

....

....

....

....

....
....
....
....
....
....
....
....
....
....
....
....
....
....

RESPOND

THINK ABOUT A CHALLENGE
YOU'RE FACING. CALL A MENTOR,
PARENT, OR GRANDPARENT TO
ASK IF THEY HAVE EXPERIENCED
SOMETHING SIMILAR. LEARN HOW
THEY OVERCAME THE SITUATION,
THEN WRITE OUT WAYS YOU
CAN USE THEIR EXPERIENCE
IN YOUR SITUATION.

▼▼▼▼▼▼▼▼

Break the Habit

For the Spirit God gave us does not make us timid,

but gives us power, love, and self-discipline.

2 TIMOTHY 1:7

The strongest athletes and most skilled musicians are those who have the discipline to train and practice, knowing that their sacrifices make them stronger. When we work to develop our spiritual habits, we put the tools and practices into place to bounce back from any challenge.

REFLECT

What is a spiritual discipline you have developed a strong habit around? What is one that you want to develop further?

....

....

....

....

....

....

....

....

....

....

....

....

....

....

....

....

....

....

....

....

....

....

....

....

....

....

....

....

....

....

....

RESPOND

DO YOU HAVE A BAD HABIT
THAT CAUSES YOU STRESS?
WRITE OUT A GAME PLAN
FOR TACKLING IT HEAD-ON
AND ASK A FRIEND FOR
MORAL AND PRAYER
SUPPORT.

WEEK 42

▼▼▼▼▼▼▼▼▼

Be Still

Be still before the LORD and wait patiently for him;

do not fret when people succeed in their ways,

when they carry out their wicked schemes.

PSALM 37:7

It's incredibly frustrating when we see people get away with bad behavior, or even benefit from their questionable choices. You may find yourself worrying about how their choices might impact you or others. But you can take heart that God is in control and we can rest in His sovereignty.

REFLECT

Is there someone in your life making choices that are harmful to herself/himself or to others? How is that situation adding to your worries?

....

....

....

....

....

....

....

SPEND AT LEAST FIVE MINUTES
A DAY THIS WEEK IN SOLITUDE
AND SILENCE. LIFT THAT PERSON'S
NAME TO GOD AND THEN BE
STILL IN HIS PRESENCE. REPEAT
THIS UNTIL YOU START TO FEEL
MORE AT PEACE ABOUT
THE SITUATION.

▼▼▼▼▼▼▼▼▼

Put It Off

Therefore do not worry about tomorrow,
for tomorrow will worry about itself. Each
day has enough trouble of its own.

MATTHEW 6:34

So many of us lament what feels like a shortage of hours on a given day, and yet we waste so much of the time we do have worrying about things that aren't in our hands instead of taking care of what's right in front of us. If we can focus on each moment in each day as the gift that it is, we can shift our whole perspective.

REFLECT

What are some things you're worried about that might happen in the future? How many of the things you're worried about relate directly to today? What would it feel like to remove the worries of tomorrow from your shoulders today?

....

....

....

....

....

....

....

....

....

....

....

....

....

....

....

....

....

....

....

....

....

....

....

....

....

....

RESPOND

ON A STICKY NOTE, WRITE
OUT THE BIGGEST FUTURE
WORRY ON YOUR MIND. STICK
IT ON TOMORROW'S DATE IN
YOUR PLANNER AND RESOLVE
NOT TO WORRY ABOUT IT UNTIL
TOMORROW. TRY REPEATING
THIS PROCESS AND OBSERVE
WHAT HAPPENS.

▼▼▼▼▼▼▼▼▼

Run Away

But you . . . flee from all this, and pursue righteousness,

godliness, faith, love, endurance and gentleness.

1 TIMOTHY 6:11

There's no law that says we're obliged to worry, yet so many
of us are slaves to the impulse. Ironically, the Bible commands
us again and again *not* to worry. Worry can inflict damage on
us, so the Bible encourages us not to do it. Instead, we are to
ruthlessly pursue righteousness, godliness, faith, love . . . and
other wonderful things.

REFLECT

How do you tackle and "flee from" other bad habits? How
might you apply those practices to eradicating worry from
your life?

....

....

....

....

....

....

....

....

....

....

....

....

....

....

....

....

....

....

....

....

....

....

....

....

....

....

....

....

....

....

RESPOND

WHEN YOU ARE OVERCOME
BY WORRY, GO FOR A WALK OR
JOG OR DO SOME OTHER ACTIVITY
LIKE WASHING DISHES OR READING
A BOOK THAT HELPS CLEAR YOUR
MIND. USE THIS PRACTICE TO
PUT DISTANCE BETWEEN YOUR
WORRIES AND YOURSELF.

▼▼▼▼▼▼▼▼▼

Get Healthy

A cheerful heart is good medicine, but a

crushed spirit dries up the bones.

PROVERBS 17:22

There's a strong connection between our minds, bodies, and souls. When we allow wrong thinking and worry to fill our minds, it can have a negative effect on our physical health. But isn't it amazing that a cheerful heart can be as good as medicine?! That healthy body can help us bounce back from stress.

REFLECT

How has worrying affected you physically? How have health issues affected your ability to deal with anxious thoughts?

....

....

....

....

....

....

....

....

....

....

....

....

....

....

....

....

....

....

....

....

....

....

....

....

....

....

....

....

RESPOND

IF YOU HAVE BEEN IGNORING
HEALTH ISSUES THAT
SUBCONSCIOUSLY TROUBLE YOU,
COMMIT TO A PLAN TO ADDRESS
THEM. FOR EXAMPLE, SEE YOUR
DOCTOR, MODIFY YOUR DIET,
GET MORE SLEEP OR FRESH
AIR, AND/OR DRINK
MORE WATER.

WEEK 46

▼▼▼▼▼▼▼▼▼

Look Outward

[I]n humility value others above yourselves,
not looking to your own interests but each
of you to the interests of the others.

PHILIPPIANS 2:3-4

When we dwell on our own problems, they seem to grow
bigger and darker and more menacing. But when we
compassionately shift our focus to the problems of others,
somehow our own seem less daunting. Not less important, but
less all-consuming.

REFLECT

Describe a time when taking care of the needs of others
helped take your mind off your own stress.

....

....

....

....

....

....

....

....

....

....

....

....

....

....

....

....

....

....

....

....

....

....

....

....

....

....

RESPOND

THINK OF TWO PEOPLE
WHO ARE GOING THROUGH A
GENUINELY DIFFICULT TIME
AND FIND A WAY TO REACH
OUT WITH SOME HELP OR
ENCOURAGEMENT
THIS WEEK.

▼▼▼▼▼▼▼▼▼

Breathe

*Jesus said, "Peace be with you! . . ." And with that he
breathed on them and said, "Receive the Holy Spirit."*

JOHN 20:21, 22

The Bible refers to the Holy Spirit as the Comforter. Since how
we breathe can affect how calm, safe, and comfortable we
feel, the idea of Jesus breathing on His followers can provide a
soothing picture of how He gave us His Holy Spirit.

REFLECT

How does remembering that God's Holy Spirit is with you help
you face difficulties?

....

....

....

....

....

....

....

....

....

....
....
....
....
....
....
....
....
....
....
....
....
....
....
....
....
....
....
....

RESPOND

SELECT TWO OR THREE
TIMES IN YOUR DAILY SCHEDULE
TO FOCUS ON YOUR BREATHING
FOR A FEW MINUTES (FOR
EXAMPLE, WHILE FOLDING
LAUNDRY OR WASHING DISHES).
AS YOU INHALE SLOWLY, THANK
GOD FOR HIS SPIRIT. AS YOU
EXHALE, LET GO OF
YOUR WORRIES.

▼▼▼▼▼▼▼▼▼

Just Ask

*Ask and it will be given to you; seek and you will
find; knock and the door will be opened to you.*

MATTHEW 7:7

Some of us seem to be hard-wired to do things on our own,
to struggle along and make do. It could be that we haven't
experienced receiving care and help from others, or it could
be a matter of pride. In our time of struggle, Jesus encourages
us to just *ask*.

REFLECT

When you feel defeated by pressures and worries, how easy
is it for you to ask for help? Why or why not? What would it
mean to you for someone to stand by your side and help? How
could help from one person or a community help you see the
other side of your challenge?

....

....

....

....

....

....

....

....

....

....

....

....

....

....

....

....

....

....

....

....

....

....

....

....

....

....

....

RESPOND

AS YOU PRAY ABOUT A
SPECIFIC SITUATION YOU'RE
STRUGGLING WITH TODAY, ASK
GOD TO HELP YOU IDENTIFY
SOMEONE YOU CAN CALL ON,
WHETHER FOR HANDS-ON HELP
OR ADVICE. REACH OUT TO
THAT PERSON WITH COURAGE
THIS WEEK.

Just Do It!

Have I not commanded you? Be strong and courageous.

Do not be afraid; do not be discouraged, for the Lord

your God will be with you wherever you go.

JOSHUA 1:9

When worry is tangled up with fear, we can feel paralyzed. What if the next step leads to failure, humiliation, danger, or loss? In such times, the best thing to do is take a leap of faith and trust God's promise to be with you always.

REFLECT

Why do you think God commands us to be courageous, rather than simply making it a suggestion or a gentle pat on the back? In what ways could you be courageous today?

....

....

....

....

....

....

....

....

....
....
....
....
....
....
....
....
....
....
....
....
....
....
....
....
....
....
....

RESPOND

CREATE A REMINDER ON
YOUR PHONE THAT SAYS
"GOD IS WITH YOU." SET IT
TO POP UP AT THE SAME
TIME EVERY DAY
THIS WEEK.

....
....
....
....
....
....
....

▼▼▼▼▼▼▼▼▼

If You Can't Sleep . . .

My eyes stay open through the watches of the

night, that I may meditate on your promises.

PSALM 119:148

One of the pitfalls of worrying is that it can keep us up at night, which just makes us tired the next day and even less able to cope with stress. Here we see King David staying awake, not to worry but to remember and reflect on God's promises.

REFLECT

When you have trouble sleeping, how do you spend that time? Are there specific routines that you fall back on to help find rest?

....

....

....

....

....

....

....

....

....

....

....

....

....

....

....

....

....

....

....

....

....

....

....

....

....

....

....

....

....

....

....

....

RESPOND

AS PART OF YOUR BEDTIME
ROUTINE, PRAY OVER YOUR
BED, YOUR PILLOW, AND YOUR
TIME OF SLEEP. ASK GOD TO
PROTECT YOUR MIND THROUGH
THE NIGHT. IF YOU DO AWAKEN
DURING THE NIGHT, FOCUS ON
PRAYING TO RELEASE YOUR
WORRIES TO GOD.

▼▼▼▼▼▼▼▼▼

Plan Ahead

For which of you, desiring to build a tower,

does not first sit down and count the cost,

whether he has enough to complete it?

LUKE 14:28 (ESV)

When our lives are chaotic and disorderly, eventually our emotions start to match. Staying organized can save not only time but also a lot of stress and heartache.

REFLECT

What have been some of the consequences you've experienced when you haven't planned ahead, kept track of details, or put things where they belong? Think of the most recent time this happened; what could you have done differently to plan ahead?

....

....

....

....

....

....

....

....

▼▼▼▼▼▼▼▼▼

Forget the Past

Therefore, if anyone is in Christ, he is a new creation.

The old has passed away; behold, the new has come.

2 CORINTHIANS 5:17

We don't worry only when we're afraid of the future. Sometimes we worry because we can't forget the past. We wonder if we've been forgiven, if we've really changed, if our past choices harmed others. God calls us to leave all of that behind us.

REFLECT

What are some regrets that linger in your heart and mind, making you feel anxious?

....

....

....

....

....

....

....

....

....

....

....

....

....

....

....

....

....

....

....

....

....

....

....

....

RESPOND

SURRENDER THE REGRETS
LISTED ABOVE TO GOD AS YOU
CROSS THEM OUT ONE AT A TIME.
DECLARE THAT THEY NO LONGER
HAVE POWER OVER YOU. CLOSE TO
EACH ONE, WRITE OUT "I AM
A NEW CREATION."

Daily
Resilience
Tracker

Remembrance is a valuable tool when recovering from challenges and moving on to face new ones. This is why the Israelites set up "Ebenezer altars" or "stones of remembrance" to mark the milestones of God's faithfulness as they journeyed through the wilderness.

As you continue your journey of building a habit of resilience, use the following pages to *jot down specific obstacles or situations you overcame and how you bounced back from them.* Allow this list to become your own written "record of remembrance" as you grow in resilience.

RESILIENCE
▼▼▼▼▼▼▼▼▼▼

January

1 ....
2 ....
3 ....
4 ....
5 ....
6 ....
7 ....
8 ....
9 ....
10 ....
11 ....
12 ....
13 ....
14 ....
15 ....
16 ....
17 ....
18 ....
19 ....
20 ....
21 ....
22 ....
23 ....
24 ....
25 ....
26 ....
27 ....
28 ....
29 ....
30 ....
31 ....

RESILIENCE

▼▼▼▼▼▼▼▼▼▼

February

1 ....
2 ....
3 ....
4 ....
5 ....
6 ....
7 ....
8 ....
9 ....
10 ....
11 ....
12 ....
13 ....
14 ....
15 ....
16 ....
17 ....
18 ....
19 ....
20 ....
21 ....
22 ....
23 ....
24 ....
25 ....
26 ....
27 ....
28 ....
29 ....

RESILIENCE
▼▼▼▼▼▼▼▼▼

March

1 ....

2 ....

3 ....

4 ....

5 ....

6 ....

7 ....

8 ....

9 ....

10 ....

11 ....

12 ....

13 ....

14 ....

15 ....

16 ....

17 ....

18 ....

19 ....

20 ....

21 ....

22 ....

23 ....

24 ....

25 ....

26 ....

27 ....

28 ....

29 ....

30 ....

31 ....

RESILIENCE

▼▼▼▼▼▼▼▼▼▼

April

1 ....

2 ....

3 ....

4 ....

5 ....

6 ....

7 ....

8 ....

9 ....

10 ....

11 ....

12 ....

13 ....

14 ....

15 ....

16 ....

17 ....

18 ....

19 ....

20 ....

21 ....

22 ....

23 ....

24 ....

25 ....

26 ....

27 ....

28 ....

29 ....

30 ....

RESILIENCE
▼▼▼▼▼▼▼▼▼

May

1 ....
2 ....
3 ....
4 ....
5 ....
6 ....
7 ....
8 ....
9 ....
10 ....
11 ....
12 ....
13 ....
14 ....
15 ....
16 ....
17 ....
18 ....
19 ....
20 ....
21 ....
22 ....
23 ....
24 ....
25 ....
26 ....
27 ....
28 ....
29 ....
30 ....
31 ....

June

1 ....
2 ....
3 ....
4 ....
5 ....
6 ....
7 ....
8 ....
9 ....
10 ....
11 ....
12 ....
13 ....
14 ....
15 ....
16 ....
17 ....
18 ....
19 ....
20 ....
21 ....
22 ....
23 ....
24 ....
25 ....
26 ....
27 ....
28 ....
29 ....
30 ....

RESILIENCE
▼▼▼▼▼▼▼▼▼

July

1 ....
2 ....
3 ....
4 ....
5 ....
6 ....
7 ....
8 ....
9 ....
10 ....
11 ....
12 ....
13 ....
14 ....
15 ....
16 ....
17 ....
18 ....
19 ....
20 ....
21 ....
22 ....
23 ....
24 ....
25 ....
26 ....
27 ....
28 ....
29 ....
30 ....
31 ....

RESILIENCE

▼▼▼▼▼▼▼▼▼

August

1 ....
2 ....
3 ....
4 ....
5 ....
6 ....
7 ....
8 ....
9 ....
10 ....
11 ....
12 ....
13 ....
14 ....
15 ....
16 ....
17 ....
18 ....
19 ....
20 ....
21 ....
22 ....
23 ....
24 ....
25 ....
26 ....
27 ....
28 ....
29 ....
30 ....
31 ....

RESILIENCE

▼▼▼▼▼▼▼▼▼

September

1 ....
2 ....
3 ....
4 ....
5 ....
6 ....
7 ....
8 ....
9 ....
10 ....
11 ....
12 ....
13 ....
14 ....
15 ....
16 ....
17 ....
18 ....
19 ....
20 ....
21 ....
22 ....
23 ....
24 ....
25 ....
26 ....
27 ....
28 ....
29 ....
30 ....

RESILIENCE

▼▼▼▼▼▼▼▼▼

October

1 ....
2 ....
3 ....
4 ....
5 ....
6 ....
7 ....
8 ....
9 ....
10 ....
11 ....
12 ....
13 ....
14 ....
15 ....
16 ....
17 ....
18 ....
19 ....
20 ....
21 ....
22 ....
23 ....
24 ....
25 ....
26 ....
27 ....
28 ....
29 ....
30 ....
31 ....

November

1 ....
2 ....
3 ....
4 ....
5 ....
6 ....
7 ....
8 ....
9 ....
10 ....
11 ....
12 ....
13 ....
14 ....
15 ....
16 ....
17 ....
18 ....
19 ....
20 ....
21 ....
22 ....
23 ....
24 ....
25 ....
26 ....
27 ....
28 ....
29 ....
30 ....

RESILIENCE

▼▼▼▼▼▼▼▼▼

December

1 ....
2 ....
3 ....
4 ....
5 ....
6 ....
7 ....
8 ....
9 ....
10 ....
11 ....
12 ....
13 ....
14 ....
15 ....
16 ....
17 ....
18 ....
19 ....
20 ....
21 ....
22 ....
23 ....
24 ....
25 ....
26 ....
27 ....
28 ....
29 ....
30 ....
31 ....

Thank you to Ann-Margret Hovsepian for all her help in creating the text for this journal.

Photograph Credits

Photographs courtesy of Stocksy United:
© Alessio Bogani, page 1; © Adrian Cotiga, page 2; © Sophia Hsin, page 8; © Helen Rushbrook, page 10; © Mark Windom, page 15; © ADDICTIVE CREATIVES, page 16; © Rialto Images, page 29; © Hannah Garvin, page 37; © Lauren Edmonds, page 38; © Treasures & Travels, page 40; © Duet Postscriptum, page 45; © Marilar Irastorza, page 65; © Melanie DeFazio, page 68; © Borislav Zhuykov, page 70; © Marilar Irastorza, page 75; © Kelly Knox, page 79; © Hannah Garvin, page 95; © Marc Tran, page 98; © Martí Sans, page 100; © Borislav Zhuykov, page 107; © Catherine MacBride, page 111; © Brad and Jen Butcher, page 117; © Aleksandra Jankovic, page 128; © Nadine Greeff, page 142.

Photographs courtesy of Shutterstock:
© Mara Ze, page 19; © vetre, page 23; © Picsfive, page 26; © Anneleven Images, page 33; © Tangerinesky, page 47; © Sonja Rachbauer, page 49; © aaltair, page 52; © TabitaZn, page 57; © Stone36, page 60; © Daria Minaeva, page 82; © ABCDstock, page 87; © ibreakstock, page 89; © Marco Montalti, page 105; © sevenke, page 112; © Daboost, page 121; © Alexxndr, page 124.

This book is not intended to replace the advice of a trained psychologist or medical professional. Readers are advised to consult a qualified professional regarding treatment. The publisher specifically disclaims liability, loss, or risk, personal or otherwise, which is incurred as a consequence, directly or indirectly, of the use or application of any of the contents of this book.

Hardcover ISBN 978-0-593-23513-3

Design by Danielle Deschenes
Photograph credits appear on page 142.

Published in the United States by WaterBrook, an imprint of Random House, a division of Penguin Random House LLC.

Ink & Willow and its tree colophon are registered trademarks of Penguin Random House LLC.

Printed in China
2021—First Edition

10 9 8 7 6 5 4 3 2 1

Special Sales
Most WaterBrook and Ink & Willow books are available at special quantity discounts when purchased in bulk by corporations, organizations, and special-interest groups. Custom imprinting or excerpting can also be done to fit special needs. For information, please email specialmarketscms @penguinrandomhouse.com.